THE Brandon Family Legacy

Preserving the Stories, Lives, and Lineage

of the Brandon Family

by

B.K. Anderson

Copyright

© 2026 by B.K. Anderson

All rights reserved.

No part of this book may be reproduced or transmitted in any form or by any means, electronic or mechanical, including photocopying, recording, or by any information storage and retrieval system, without permission in writing from the author, except for brief quotations used in reviews or scholarly works.

This book is a work of family history and remembrance. Every effort has been made to ensure accuracy. Any errors or omissions are unintentional.

ISBN# 9798993853178

Printed in the United States of America.

Dedication

To the past, present, and future members of the Brandon family—

to those whose stories are remembered,

and to those yet to come.

This book was created to preserve the stories, names, and connections of the Brandon family.

Family history is more than dates and records. It is made of lives lived, journeys taken, and memories passed down—sometimes quietly, sometimes imperfectly, but always with meaning.

My hope is that this book serves as both a record and a memory. May it help current and future generations understand where they came from and feel connected to those who came before them.

Author's Note

How to Use This Book

This book may be read from beginning to end or used as a reference.

Names, dates, and family connections are presented to help preserve accuracy, while stories and recollections offer context and meaning. Readers are encouraged to add notes, memories, or corrections, so that this legacy may continue to grow.

Personal Introduction and Purpose

I want to begin by sharing who I am and why I felt called to do this book, because this story comes from personal experience, long familiarity, and deep respect.

I have known **Buckshot Brandon, Buck Brandon, and Little Buck Brandon** for most of my adult life. These were not brief or distant connections. Our lives crossed through years of work, shared time, and everyday conversation, the kind of connections that are built slowly and honestly.

I worked alongside **Little Buck, Bruce Brandon, for over thirty years**. When you spend that much time working with someone, you come to know their character, their work ethic, and the way they treat others. Bruce was someone I respected not just as a coworker, but as a steady presence over decades of working life.

I to work a harvest season with **his father**, which gave me another perspective on the family. Through that experience, I saw the same values carried across generations—commitment to work, pride in doing things right, and respect for others. I remember **Raymond Sr. coming by the**

workplace to talk with his son, Raymond Jr., Bruce's father. Those moments may seem small, but they mattered. They showed the continuity of family, the connection between generations, and the quiet strength of relationships that extended beyond the home and into daily life.

The reason I wanted to do this book is simple. I have known the Brandon family for many years, and I have a deep respect for the whole family. This book is not written from hearsay or secondhand accounts, but from lived experience and long familiarity. It is written because stories like these deserve to be preserved stories of people who worked hard, showed up consistently, and lived their lives with dignity.

This is not a book meant to glorify or embellish, nor to rewrite history. It is written as an act of respect and appreciation. Too often, the stories of families like the Brandon's are never written down, and when they are lost, something important is lost with them. I wanted to help make sure that did not happen here.

This book is my way of honoring a family that has been part of my life for many years, and of preserving their story with honesty and care.

Brian Keith Anderson

TABLE OF CONTENTS

Front Matter

Title Page 1

Copyright 2

Dedication 3

Author's Note 4

Personal Introduction and Purpose 5

PART I — PERSONAL & CONTEMPORARY FAMILY

Bruce Brandon — A Personal Profile 10

Descendants Line of the Brandon Family 32

PART II — THE DIRECT ANCESTRAL LINE

The Line of Raymond "Buckshot" Brandon 33

Monroe A. Brandon 33

Edmond Brandon 41

Abraham Brandon 50

Cornelius Brandon 62

George B. Brandon 86

George William Brandon Sr. 91

John Richard Brandon (Founding Ancestor) 101

PART III — CLOSING

From the Old World to the Present Day 108

The Brandon Line Continues 109

Bruce Brandon – A Personal Profile

Bruce DeWayne Brandon

This book opens with Bruce Brandon because his life and presence are woven through both my own story and the wider Brandon family story I am preserving here. I worked alongside Bruce for more than forty years, sharing seasons of work, change, and quiet endurance. Over that time, I came to know him not just as a colleague, but as someone whose steadiness, memory, and character helped many of us anchors.

Bruce carried with him a deep sense of responsibility to family and community. He did not seek spotlight, yet his influence was felt in the way he showed up — consistently, calmly, and with care for those around him. In conversations, in work, and in ordinary moments of life, he reflected the kind of grounded strength that holds families together across generations.

The photographs he has shared for this book are more than images; they are doorways into memory — reminders of who came before, what was built, and what endures. Through them, and through his own recollections, Bruce helps keep the Brandon lineage alive not as dates on a page, but as living history.

This profile honors him as a witness to much of that history and as a bridge between the past and the present.

I worked with Bruce until my retirement. We shared many good years together, and those years left a deep mark on my life. Bruce was more than a co-worker — he is a loyal friend, a friend for life.

In many ways, Bruce is the reason I began my ancestral work. While researching my own family cemeteries and tracing my lines, I was also working on my Anderson Legacy books. During that time, I decided to do Bruce's line as well and place a copy of his family history in the library. That decision grew into this book.

Our working life together spanned decades. We first worked side-by-side at Gold Kist, Inc. in Manchester Grain Elevator. When Gold Kist left Kokomo Grain, we moved with the work to Kokomo, which had a contract with Jack Daniel Distillery and handled grain for their whiskey. At the same time, Kokomo also handled George Dickel's grain.

We worked together for more than thirty years. When Kokomo left, we both went to Woodall Grain Company, which had purchased Kokomo's elevators. I continued to work with Bruce there until I retired in 2024.

Our days were long — harvest seasons were exhausting — but there was purpose in the work. Farmers depended on us, and we depended on each other. Bruce eventually became the manager at Woodall Grain, now one of the largest grain elevators in the mid-South.

I first met Bruce when he was around sixteen. His father, Buck, worked with me at Manchester Grain Elevator. Bruce would come after school to help. Even then, he was hardworking and steady.

Bruce's father, Buck Brandon, also operated his own business selling produce at the Nashville Farmers Market. He sold watermelons and cantaloupes, and they were loaded by hand, Bruce went with his father to Florida, and his father brought produce, and hand loaded them one at a time. Bringing them back to sell. Buck's father Buckshot — who is also mentioned in this book — ran a spot inside the market, and that was what he was doing when I first met him.

When Bruce graduated high school, he came to work full-time with us at Gold Kist. From there, his career in grain grew into a lifetime of leadership, responsibility, and respect in the agricultural community.

Because of this long friendship — and because of the years we spent side by side — this book came to be.

— **B.K. Anderson**

Back Left to right: Buck, John, Siba, Buckshot, Jimmy Harmon

Front Left to right: Gerdine Adcock, Eunice Harmon, Joyce Trail

Gravestone of Buckshot and Siba

Buckshot, John, Buck Brandon

Bruce Brandon owes this truck it was Buckshot. He is restoring it at this time. When Buckshot purchased this truck, he had Bruce with him and let him drive it home from dealer, he was 16 at the time.

Siba McCullough and Raymond B Brandon

Raymond B. Brandon, Sr., was born on **January 19, 1919**, in **Cannon County, Tennessee**, during a time when rural communities were closely knit and family ties ran deep. Growing up in Middle Tennessee, Raymond witnessed a period of momentous change in the nation and carried the steady values of his upbringing throughout his life.

He remained connected to the region that shaped him, and his life reflected the rhythms of Tennessee family lifework, responsibility, and devotion to home. Raymond passed away on **September 11, 1983**, in **Manchester, Coffee County, Tennessee**, where he was laid to rest among the people and places familiar to him.

His life stands as part of the enduring foundation of the **Brandon family legacy**, remembered through the generations that followed.

Siba M. McCullough Brandon was born on **January 7, 1920**, in **Coffee County, Tennessee**. Raised in Middle Tennessee, she came of age in a period defined by resilience, family devotion, and strong community bonds—values she carried throughout her life.

Siba spent much of her life rooted in **Coffee County**, where home, family, and continuity were central. She lived a long life marked by dedication to those she loved and passed away on **August 31, 2013**, in **Manchester, Coffee County, Tennessee**.

Through her life and legacy, **Siba M. McCullough Brandon** remains an enduring part of the Brandon family story, remembered with respect and gratitude by the generations who followed.

Children:

Eunice Brandon was born **about 1937** in **Coffee County, Tennessee**. Growing up in Middle Tennessee, she became part of the next generation, carrying forward the Brandon family name and traditions rooted in the region.

As a living member of the family, Eunice represents the continuing legacy of **Raymond B. Brandon, Sr.,** and **Siba M. McCullough Brandon**, connecting past generations with those yet to come.

Eunice Brandon

Spouse:

Clayton Harmon

Born **3 May 1931** in **Coffee County, Tennessee**, Clayton Harmon grew up during a period marked by the lingering effects of the Great Depression and the approach of World War II. Raised in a rural Tennessee community, he experienced firsthand the values of hard work, family responsibility, and perseverance that defined life in Coffee County during the mid-20th century.

Clayton spent most of his life rooted in **Coffee County**, maintaining close ties to the Manchester area and the surrounding countryside. Like many men of his generation, his life reflected steady commitment—to family, community, and the rhythms of everyday work that sustained local life.

He married **Eunice Brandon**, uniting two long-standing Coffee County families. Their marriage strengthened family bonds within the Brandon lineage and carried forward traditions of kinship and mutual support. Together, they shared a life grounded in place, family connection, and community continuity.

Clayton Harmon passed away on **19 March 2016** in **Manchester, Coffee County, Tennessee**, leaving behind a legacy remembered by family and those who knew him. His life stands as part of the enduring story of the Brandon family's presence in Coffee County—one generation among many who shaped its history through quiet dedication and lasting ties

Raymond Brandon Jr.

Raymond Brandon Jr. was born on **October 21, 1939**, in **Bedford County, Tennessee**. As part of the next generation of the Brandon family, he grew up during a period of recovery of post-Depression and wartime change, shaped by the values and traditions passed down from his parents.

Raymond spent his life in Tennessee, maintaining strong ties to the region that had long been home to his family. He passed away on **July 19, 2016**, in **Murfreesboro, Rutherford County, Tennessee**, leaving behind a legacy rooted in family continuity and remembrance.

Spouse:

Francis Ruth Winton

Born **20 April 1936** in **Coffee County, Tennessee**, Francis Ruth Winton came of age during a time of profound change in rural Tennessee, shaped by post-Depression resilience and the close-knit values of community and family life. Raised in Coffee County, she was part of a generation that bridged traditional ways of living with a rapidly modernizing world.

She married **Raymond B. Brandon**, becoming his lifelong partner and an integral part of the Brandon family legacy. As wife and mother, Francis Ruth helped anchor the family through daily life, nurturing relationships, traditions, and the continuity of home. Her role within the family reflected quiet strength, devotion, and steadfast presence—qualities often carried forward by those who knew her best.

Francis Ruth spent her life deeply connected to **Manchester and Coffee County**, where family, faith, and community shaped everyday experience. Her influence lived not only in her household but also in the enduring bonds she helped sustain among extended family members.

She passed away on **15 July 1991** in **Manchester, Coffee County, Tennessee**, leaving a legacy remembered through the family she helped build and the generations that followed. Her life remains an essential chapter in the story of the Brandon family in Coffee County.

Children:

Bruce Dewayne Brandon: Born in 1962

Cindy Lynn Brandon: Born in 1964

John Henry Brandon

John Henry Brandon was born on **July 20, 1941**, in **Bedford County, Tennessee**. Growing up in a family deeply rooted in Middle Tennessee, he was part of a generation shaped by the years surrounding World War II and the enduring strength of close-knit communities.

John Henry spent much of his life connected to Bedford County, the place of both his birth and passing. He died on **March 13, 2009**, in **Bedford County, Tennessee**, leaving a lasting place in the Brandon family lineage and in the memories of those who knew him.

Spouse:

Sarah Helena Lowe

Born **31 July 1941** in **Bedford County, Tennessee**, Sarah Helena Lowe grew up in Middle Tennessee during a period shaped by wartime uncertainty and post-war renewal. Raised in a region rich with agricultural traditions and close-knit communities, she carried forward values of family devotion, resilience, and care for others throughout her life.

She married **John Henry Brandon**, joining the Lowe and Brandon families and becoming an important part of the Brandon family lineage. As wife and mother, Sarah Helena played a significant role in maintaining family bonds, offering steady support, and nurturing the home life that sustained those around her. Her presence reflected strength, warmth, and commitment across the years of their shared life.

Sarah Helena spent much of her life in Tennessee, later residing in the **Murfreesboro** area. Her life bridged counties and generations yet remained grounded in the traditions and relationships that defined Middle Tennessee family life.

She passed away on **27 January 2020** in **Murfreesboro, Rutherford County, Tennessee**, leaving behind a legacy of love, dedication, and family continuity. Her memory endures through the lives she touched, and the generations connected to her care.

Gerdine Brandon

Gerdine Brandon was born **about 1944** in **Tennessee**, growing up as part of a generation shaped by post–World War II change and strong family bonds. As a member of the Brandon family, she shared traditions and connections that defined life in Middle Tennessee.

Gerdine remained closely tied to her home state throughout her life and passed away in **2024** in **Manchester, Tennessee**. Her life is remembered as part of the continuing Brandon family story, honored by those who knew and loved her.

Ed Randall Brandon

Ed Randall Brandon was born on **March 22, 1945**, in **Beechgrove, Coffee County, Tennessee**. Raised in a close-knit Middle Tennessee community, he was part of the generation that came of age in the years following World War II, shaped by family, place, and tradition.

Ed Randall spent his life intricately connected to Beechgrove, the community of both his birth and passing. He died on **September 20, 2014**, in **Beechgrove, Coffee County, Tennessee**, leaving behind a place of honor within the Brandon family lineage and the memories of those who knew him

Joyce Brandon

Joyce Brandon was born in **Coffee County, Tennessee**, and grew up as part of the Brandon family rooted in Middle Tennessee. As a member of the next generation, she shares in the traditions, values, and family connections established by those who came before her.

As a living member of the family, Joyce represents the continuing and living legacy of the **Brandon family**, linking its history to the present day.

Joyce married: Bobby Trail

Descendants Line of the Brandon Family

1. Bruce D. 1962 --- Cindy L. 1964

2. Raymond B. Jr.-- 1939—2016

3. Raymond B. – 1919--1983

4. Monroe A. – 1875—1954

5. Edmond – 1838—1921

6. Abraham – 1811—1896

7. Cornelius – 1783—1852

8. George W. Jr – 1732—1826

9. George W. Sr. – 1702—1772

10. John R. Brandon – 1672 1716

The Brandon family line in Coffee and surrounding counties reflects generations of steady lives rooted in Tennessee soil. What follows is the direct ancestral line leading to Raymond Brandon Sr., preserving the names and places that shaped the family long before his own lifetime.

The Line Of; Raymond Buckshot Brandon

Monroe A. Brandon

Monroe A. Brandon

- **Born:** January 21, 1875 — Cannon County, Tennessee
- **Died:** December 8, 1954 — Beech Grove, Coffee County, Tennessee

Monroe A. Brandon represents a foundational generation in the Brandon family's Tennessee history. Born in Cannon County during the post-Civil War era, he lived through a period of major transition as rural communities shifted from nineteenth-century traditions into the modern twentieth century.

By adulthood, Monroe had established his life in Beech Grove, Coffee County, Tennessee, where he became part of a stable, multi-generational family presence. His years there marked the continuation of the Brandon line in Middle Tennessee and laid the groundwork for the generations that followed.

Wife

Sarah Bell Wilson

- **Born:** December 11, 1887 — Cannon County, Tennessee

- **Died:** July 31, 1951 — Beech Grove, Coffee County, Tennessee

Sarah Bell Wilson shared Monroe's Cannon County origins and later life in Beech Grove, Coffee County. Together, Monroe and Sarah represent a stable family unit whose lives bridged between the nineteenth and twentieth centuries, providing continuity and grounding for the Brandon family line.

Children of Monroe A. Brandon and Sarah Bell Wilson

Gracey C. Brandon

1. **Gracey C. Brandon**
   - **Born:** 1904 — Tennessee
   - **Died:** Unknown

Gracey C. Brandon belongs to the generation born at the beginning of the twentieth century, a period of rapid change in rural Tennessee. Further details of Gracey's adult life may be added as records become available.

Hoyt Herbert Brandon

Hoyt Herbert Brandon

- **Born:** November 12, 1904 — Tennessee
- **Died:** November 21, 1981 — Coffee County, Tennessee

Hoyt Herbert Brandon was born at the opening of the twentieth century, a time when rural Tennessee families were transitioning into a new era shaped by industry, modernization, and change. Raised within the established Brandon family of Middle Tennessee, Hoyt carried forward the values and continuity set in place by earlier generations.

He spent much of his life in Coffee County, Tennessee, where the Brandon name remained closely tied to the local community. His lifespan bridged two centuries, connecting the agricultural roots of his parents' generation with the evolving world experienced by his children and grandchildren.

Thurman B. Brandon

Thurman B. Brandon

- **Born:** 1908 — Tennessee
- **Died:** 1990 — Manchester, Coffee County, Tennessee

Thurman B. Brandon was born into the Brandon family during the early years of the twentieth century, a generation shaped by hard work, close-knit communities, and deep ties to Middle Tennessee. His life spanned decades of change, from the agricultural rhythms of rural Tennessee to the modern era that followed.

He lived in Manchester, Coffee County, Tennessee, where the Brandon family name remained well known and respected. Thurman's years reflect continuity and presence, linking the earlier Brandon generations with those that came after his.

Alvin H. Brandon

Alvin H. Brandon

- **Born:** May 20, 1910 — Tennessee
- **Died:** August 1982 — Manchester, Coffee County, Tennessee, United States of America

Alvin H. Brandon was born into the Brandon family in the early twentieth century, a time when Middle Tennessee communities were tightly bound by family, work, and shared traditions. Growing up in the shadow of earlier Brandon generations, Alvin's life reflects continuity and stability within Coffee County.

He lived in Manchester, Tennessee, where the Brandon family maintained long-standing ties. Alvin's years spanned a period of meaningful change, yet his life remained grounded in the same region that had anchored his family for generations.

Jessie T. Brandon

Jessie T. Brandon

- **Born:** 1913 — Tennessee
- **Died:** 1991 — Beech Grove, Coffee County, Tennessee

Jessie T. Brandon was born into the Brandon family during a period when Middle Tennessee communities were deeply rooted in land, family, and tradition. Growing up in the early twentieth century, Jessie's life reflects the steady presence of the Brandon family in Coffee County across generations.

Jessie spent later years in Beech Grove, Tennessee, the same community where earlier Brandon generations had established their home. This continuity of place underscores the lasting family ties that define the Brandon legacy.

Raymond B. Brandon Sr.

Raymond B. Brandon Sr.

- **Born:** January 19, 1919 — Cannon County, Tennessee
- **Died:** September 11, 1983 — Manchester, Coffee County, Tennessee

Raymond B. Brandon Sr. was born in Cannon County, Tennessee, into a long-established Middle Tennessee family. As a son of Monroe A. Brandon and Sarah Bell Wilson, he grew up within a household shaped by stability, tradition, and deep local roots.

By adulthood, Raymond Sr. lived in Manchester, Coffee County, Tennessee, where he became part of the generation that carried the Brandon family through the mid-twentieth century. His life bridged the older rural world of his parents with the changing landscape experienced by his children and grandchildren.

*The following ancestral record traces the direct family line leading to Monroe A. Brandon, preserving the names and lives that shaped the Brandon family before his generation

Edmond Brandon

Edmond Brandon

- **Born:** April 5, 1838 — Cannon County, Tennessee
- **Died:** October 31, 1921 — Rutherford County, Tennessee

Edmond Brandon represents an earlier foundational generation of the Brandon family in Middle Tennessee. Born in Cannon County in the antebellum period, his life spanned some of the most transformative years in American history, including the Civil War and Reconstruction.

Through endurance and continuity, Edmond Brandon carried the family line forward into the late nineteenth century. His son, Monroe A. Brandon, would later establish the Brandon family's long-term presence in Coffee County, Tennessee, continuing the legacy begun during Edmond's lifetime.

Wife:

Cynthia Matilda Mitchell

Cynthia Matilda Mitchell

- **Born:** 1839 — Tennessee
- **Died:** January 1, 1918 — Cannon County, Tennessee, United States of America

Cynthia Matilda Mitchell belonged to a generation of Tennessee women whose lives were shaped by family, resilience, and continuity through the nineteenth century. Living through the Civil War era and into the early twentieth century, she represents the maternal line that carried stability and tradition within the Brandon family.

As the wife of Edmond Brandon, Cynthia was the mother of Monroe A. Brandon and played a vital role in sustaining the family during a period of profound national and regional change.

Siblings:

James Thomas Brandon

James Thomas Brandon

- **Born:** November 8, 1864 — Bradyville, Cannon County, Tennessee, United States of America
- **Died:** October 19, 1934 — Franklin County, Tennessee, United States of America

James Thomas Brandon was born during the final year of the Civil War in Bradyville, Cannon County, Tennessee. His life spanned a period of recovery and rebuilding in Middle Tennessee, extending into the early twentieth century as families adapted to changing economic and social conditions.

His movement from Cannon County into Franklin County reflects the gradual regional shifts common among Tennessee families of his generation, while maintaining close ties to the Brandon family's established roots.

John Granville Brandon

John Granville Brandon

- **Born:** March 1867 — Tennessee
- **Died:** Unknown

John Granville Brandon was born in Tennessee during the Reconstruction era, a period when families were rebuilding and reestablishing stability following the Civil War. His life falls within the same generational time as other members of the Brandon family associated with Cannon County and surrounding areas.

While details of his later years remain limited, his inclusion preserves an important name within the Brandon lineage and allows for future clarification as additional records are discovered.

Haney Brandon

Haney Brandon

- **Born:** 1869 — Tennessee
- **Died:** Unknown

Haney Brandon was born in Tennessee during the late Reconstruction era, a time when Middle Tennessee families were re-establishing stability following the Civil War. Haney's lifetime aligns with the same generational tier as other Brandon family members associated with Cannon County and surrounding areas.

Although limited records are presently available, preserving Haney's name within the family narrative ensures continuity and allows for future clarification as additional documentation is discovered.

Jennie Brandon

Jennie Brandon

- **Born:** 1871
- **Died:** 1947

Jennie Brandon was born in the early 1870s, part of the Brandon family generation that came of age during the late nineteenth century in Tennessee. Her lifetime spanned a period of steady transition, as rural family life gradually shifted into the modern twentieth century.

Though fewer details are presently available, Jennie's inclusion preserves an important member of the Brandon family and helps complete the picture of this generation connected to the ancestral line leading to Monroe A. Brandon.

Mattie C. Brandon

Mattie C. Brandon

- **Born:** May 21, 1872 — Cannon County, Tennessee, United States of America

- **Died:** August 30, 1957 — Murfreesboro, Rutherford County, Tennessee, United States of America

Mattie C. Brandon was born in Cannon County during the Reconstruction era and lived well into the mid-twentieth century. Her life reflects the endurance and continuity of Tennessee families whose roots extended across multiple counties while remaining connected to their place of origin.

Mattie's later years in Murfreesboro, Rutherford County, suggest family or community ties that extended beyond Cannon County, while still remaining within the Middle Tennessee region that anchored the Brandon family for generations.

Monroe A. Brandon

Monroe A. Brandon

- **Born:** January 21, 1875 — Cannon County, Tennessee
- **Died:** December 8, 1954 — Beech Grove, Coffee County, Tennessee

Monroe A. Brandon stands as the pivotal link between the nineteenth-century Brandon ancestors of Cannon County and the twentieth-century Brandon families established in Coffee County. Born during the Reconstruction era, Monroe came of age as Middle Tennessee families transitioned from post-war recovery into a period of stability and growth.

By adulthood, Monroe had settled in Beech Grove, Coffee County, where he established a lasting family presence. His life bridged generations, carrying forward the legacy of his parents while laying the foundation for the Brandon families who followed, including Raymond B. Brandon Sr.

Rosey Brandon

Rosey Brandon

- **Born:** 1880 — Tennessee
- **Died:** Unknown

Rosey Brandon was born in Tennessee in the late nineteenth century, part of the generation that followed the Civil War and Reconstruction years. Her life aligns with the Brandon family members who came of age during a period of renewed stability and continuity in Middle Tennessee.

Although details of her later life remain limited, preserving Rosey's name within the family record ensures that her place in the Brandon lineage is not lost and allows for future additions as records or family knowledge emerge.

*The individuals recorded in this generation represent the earliest documented roots of the Brandon family in Rutherford County, Tennessee, laying the foundation upon which later generations would build.

Abraham Brandon

Abraham Brandon

- **Born:** 1811 — Rutherford County, Tennessee, United States
- **Died:** 1896 — Rutherford County, Tennessee, United States

Abraham Brandon represents an early nineteenth-century generation of the Brandon family rooted in Rutherford County, Tennessee. Born during the early years of statehood, his life spanned a formative period in Tennessee history, marked by settlement, agricultural development, and the growth of established family communities.

As the father of Edmond Brandon, Abraham stands at the head of the known ancestral line leading to Monroe A. Brandon and the later Brandon families of Cannon and Coffee Counties. His long residence in Rutherford County reflects the geographic foundation from which subsequent generations would branch outward.

Wife

Ruth B. Perry

Ruth B. Perry

- **Born:** 1822 — Tennessee, United States
- **Died:** September 1850 — Cannon County, Tennessee

Ruth B. Perry belonged to the generation of Tennessee women whose lives were shaped by family, endurance, and the demands of early rural life. Her early death in Cannon County marked a brief but important chapter in the Brandon family story, preceding the westward and generational movement that followed through her children.

Children:

Edmond Brandon

Edmond Brandon

- **Born:** April 5, 1838 — Cannon County, Tennessee
- **Died:** October 31, 1921 — Rutherford County, Tennessee

Edmond Brandon represents a pivotal nineteenth-century generation of the Brandon family in Middle Tennessee. Born in Cannon County before the Civil War, his life spanned some of the most transformative years in

American history, including the war itself and the extended period of Reconstruction that followed.

Through resilience and continuity, Edmond carried the Brandon family line forward during a time of national upheaval and regional change. His later years in Rutherford County reflect the gradual movement of the family within Middle Tennessee while maintaining deep roots in the land and communities that shaped them.

Edmond Brandon stands as the generational bridge between the early Brandon settlers of the region and the later families who would establish long-term roots in Cannon and Coffee Counties.

Sarah Brandon

Sarah Brandon

- **Born:** 1839
- **Died:** Unknown

Sarah Brandon was born in the late 1830s, placing her within the same generational time as Edmond Brandon and other early members of the

Brandon family in Middle Tennessee. Her life unfolded during a period marked by settlement, family formation, and the challenges of nineteenth-century rural life.

While limited records are currently available, preserving Sarah's name within the Brandon family record ensures that her place in the lineage is acknowledged and allows for future clarification as additional documentation or family knowledge emerges.

James Brandon

James Brandon

- **Born:** 1840
- **Died:** Unknown

James Brandon was born in 1840, placing him within the mid-nineteenth-century generation of the Brandon family in Tennessee. His lifetime coincided with a period of settlement, family growth, and increasing strain leading up to the Civil War, followed by years of rebuilding and adjustment.

Although limited documentation is presently available, James Brandon's inclusion preserves an important name within the family record and maintains continuity within the Brandon lineage until further records can clarify his role more precisely.

Abraham Brandon (born 1841)

Abraham Brandon

- **Born:** 1841
- **Died:** Unknown

Abraham Brandon, born in 1841, belongs to the mid-nineteenth-century generation of the Brandon family in Tennessee. His birth places him within the same generational tier as Edmond Brandon and other family members who lived through the years surrounding the Civil War and Reconstruction.

Because his dates differ from **Abraham Brandon (1811–1896)**, this entry represents a **separate individual**, a later relative within the extended Brandon family rather than the patriarch already documented. Preserving this distinction prevents confusion and ensures accuracy within the family record.

Mary Brandon

Mary Brandon

- **Born:** 1845
- **Died:** May 16, 1920

Mary Brandon was born in the mid-1840s, placing her within the Brandon family generation that lived through the Civil War era and into the early twentieth century. Her lifetime reflects the endurance and continuity of

Tennessee families who experienced profound national change while maintaining strong family and community ties.

Her death in 1920 marks the close of a life that bridged two centuries, connecting the early Brandon generations with those who followed in the modern era

George Brandon

George Brandon

- **Born:** Unknown
- **Died:** Unknown

George Brandon is recorded as a member of the Brandon family whose life details remain undocumented. While specific dates and locations are not presently known, his inclusion preserves an important family name within the Brandon lineage and acknowledges his place among earlier generations.

Recording individuals with limited information is an essential part of family history work. It ensures that names are not lost and leaves space for future discovery as additional records or family knowledge become available.

Nancy Jane Helton

Nancy Jane Helton

- **Born:** 1824
- **Died:** 1898

Nancy Jane Helton belonged to the early nineteenth-century generation of Middle Tennessee families whose lives were shaped by settlement, family responsibility, and endurance through times of change. Her lifetime spanned the antebellum period, the Civil War, and the years of recovery that followed.

As the **second wife of Abraham Brandon (1811–1896)**, Nancy Jane Helton became part of the Brandon family after the death of his first wife, Ruth B. Perry. Through this marriage, she contributed to the continuity and stability of the Brandon household during the later years of Abraham Brandon's life.

Family Connection

- **Husband:** Abraham Brandon (1811–1896)
- **Role:** Second wife

Abraham Brandon (born 1851)

Abraham Brandon

- **Born:** 1851
- **Died:** Unknown

Abraham Brandon, born in 1851, belongs to the mid-nineteenth-century generation of the Brandon family in Tennessee. His birth places him in the period just before the Civil War, a time when family structures and communities were undergoing significant strain and change.

Because his birth year differs from both **Abraham Brandon (1811–1896)** and **Abraham Brandon (born 1841)**, this entry represents a **separate individual** within the extended Brandon family. Recording him independently preserves accuracy and prevents the merging of identities across generations.

Arch Brandon

Arch Brandon

- **Born:** 1854 — Tennessee, United States
- **Died:** Unknown

Arch Brandon was born in Tennessee in the mid-1850s, placing him within the Brandon family generation that lived through the Civil War era and into the period of Reconstruction. His lifetime aligns with other Brandon family members whose early years were shaped by national conflict and later rebuilding in Middle Tennessee.

Although specific details of his adult life are not yet documented, preserving Arch Brandon's name ensures continuity within the Brandon family record and allows for future clarification as additional records or family knowledge emerge.

Third Wife:

Sarah Ann Gatlin

Sarah Ann Gatlin

- **Born:** April 30, 1815
- **Died:** January 1, 1852

Sarah Ann Gatlin was born in the early nineteenth century, a period marked by settlement and family formation in Tennessee. Her life spanned the antebellum years and ended shortly before the midpoint of the century, a time when many families faced hardship, illness, and loss.

Although limited records are currently available, preserving Sarah Ann Gatlin's name within family history ensures her place is acknowledged and allows for future clarification as additional documentation or family knowledge emerges.

James Knox Polk Brandon

James Knox Polk Brandon

- **Born:** Unknown
- **Died:** Unknown

James Knox Polk Brandon is recorded as a member of the Brandon family whose life details are presently undocumented. His name reflects the nineteenth-century naming tradition common in Tennessee families, often honoring national figures of the era, which help place him within an early or mid-nineteenth-century context.

Although specific dates and locations are not yet known, preserving his full name within the family record ensures that this individual is not lost to time and allows for future confirmation as additional records or family knowledge become known.

Abraham's father:

Cornelius Brandon

Cornelius Brandon

- **Born:** 1783 — Rowan County, North Carolina, United States
- **Died:** December 11, 1852 — Cannon County, Tennessee, United States

Cornelius Brandon represents an earlier generation of the Brandon family whose life reflects the movement of families from North Carolina into Middle Tennessee during the late eighteenth and early nineteenth centuries. Born in Rowan County, North Carolina, he lived during a period of westward migration, settlement, and the establishment of new communities beyond the original colonies.

By adulthood, Cornelius had settled in what would become Cannon County, Tennessee, where he spent his later years. His life bridges the transition from colonial-era America into the early years of Tennessee statehood and marks a foundational step in the Brandon family's long presence in the region.

Mary Phoebe Tennison

Mary Phoebe Tennison

- **Born:** 1787 — Edgecombe County, North Carolina, United States
- **Died:** January 1866 — Burt, Cannon County, Tennessee, United States

Mary Phoebe Tennison belongs to the generation of women whose lives traced the early movement of families from North Carolina into Tennessee. Born in Edgecombe County, North Carolina, she later settled in Middle Tennessee, where she spent her later years in Cannon County.

As the wife of Cornelius Brandon, Mary Phoebe was part of the foundational family unit that carried the Brandon line from the Carolinas into Tennessee during the early nineteenth century. Her lifespan bridged the colonial period, early American settlement, and the Civil War era, reflecting endurance and continuity across generations.

James Adams Brandon

James Adams Brandon

- **Born:** May 26, 1806 — Rutherford County, Tennessee, United States
- **Died:** April 16, 1894 — Nolan County, Texas, United States

James Adams Brandon represents a nineteenth-century generation of the Brandon family shaped by migration, expansion, and settlement beyond Middle Tennessee. Born in Rutherford County during the early years of Tennessee statehood, his life reflects the movement of families westward as new territories opened for opportunity and settlement.

Later in life, James Adams Brandon relocated to Texas, where he spent his final years in Nolan County. His journey from Tennessee to Texas marks a significant branch in the broader Brandon family story and reflects the broader American pattern of westward movement during the nineteenth century.

James Adams Brandon

Jane Brandon

Jane Brandon

- **Born:** March 9, 1808 — Rutherford County, Tennessee, United States

- **Died:** November 14, 1847 — Burt, Cannon County, Tennessee, United States

Jane Brandon was born in Rutherford County, Tennessee, during the early years of statehood and lived her life during a period of settlement and family formation in Middle Tennessee. Her death in Cannon County places her firmly within the same regional movement that shaped the early Brandon family generations.

As the wife of **James Adams Brandon**, Jane belonged to the generation that carried the Brandon family line forward during the first half of the nineteenth century, bridging the transition from early Tennessee settlement into the generations that followed.

Joseph L. Brandon

Joseph L. Brandon

- **Born:** About 1810 — Rutherford County, Tennessee, United States
- **Died:** 1844 — Sumner County, Tennessee, United States

Joseph L. Brandon belongs to the early nineteenth-century generation of the Brandon family in Tennessee. Born in Rutherford County around 1810, his life unfolded during the formative years of statehood, settlement, and family expansion across Middle Tennessee.

His death in Sumner County in 1844 reflects the movement of Brandon family members within the region during this period, as families established new homes while remaining connected through kinship and shared origins.

Elizabeth Brandon

Elizabeth Brandon

- **Born:** 1813 — Rutherford County, Tennessee, United States
- **Died:** 1853 — Cannon County, Tennessee, United States

Elizabeth Brandon belongs to the early nineteenth-century generation of the Brandon family rooted in Middle Tennessee. Born in Rutherford County during the early years of Tennessee statehood, her life reflects the movement of families into Cannon County as communities expanded and settled.

Her death in Cannon County places her firmly within the same regional pattern shared by other Brandon family members of this generation, marking continuity of place during a period of family growth and transition.

Andrew Brandon

Andrew Brandon

- **Born:** 1815 — Rutherford County, Tennessee, United States
- **Died:** Unknown

Andrew Brandon belongs to the early nineteenth-century generation of the Brandon family in Middle Tennessee. Born in Rutherford County during the early years of Tennessee's statehood, his life aligns with other Brandon family members whose lives unfolded during a period of settlement, migration, and family expansion across the region.

Although details of his later life remain undocumented, preserving Andrew Brandon's name ensures continuity within the Brandon family record and leaves room for future clarification as additional records or family knowledge become available.

Christopher Columbus Brandon

Christopher Columbus Brandon

- **Born:** 1812 — Rutherford County, Tennessee, United States
- **Died:** February 1, 1904 — Swifton, Jackson County, Arkansas, United States

Christopher Columbus Brandon was born in Rutherford County, Tennessee, during the early years of statehood and lived well into the opening years of the twentieth century. His lifetime spanned an extraordinary period of American history, including westward expansion, the Civil War, Reconstruction, and the dawn of the modern era.

His later residence and death in Jackson County, Arkansas, reflect the broader migration patterns of Brandon family members who moved beyond Tennessee in search of land, opportunity, and stability. His long life connects the early Tennessee generations of the Brandon family to later branches that extended into neighboring states.

John Ellis Brandon

JOHN ELLIS BRANDON, 7th Child of Cornelius & Mary (Tennison) Brandon

John Ellis Brandon

- **Born:** 1815 — Rutherford County, Tennessee, United States
- **Died:** December 9, 1852 — Burt, Cannon County, Tennessee, United States

John Ellis Brandon was born in Rutherford County during the early years of Tennessee's statehood and lived during a period marked by settlement, family growth, and regional movement into Cannon County. His death in Burt, Cannon County, places him firmly within the same geographic transition seen among other early Brandon family members of this generation.

Though his life was brief, John Ellis Brandon's record contributes to the broader picture of the Brandon family's early nineteenth-century presence in Middle Tennessee.

David G. Brandon

David G. Brandon

- **Born:** July 24, 1816 — Rutherford County, Tennessee, United States
- **Died:** March 2, 1901 — Bradyville, Cannon County, Tennessee, United States

David G. Brandon was born in Rutherford County, Tennessee, during the early years of statehood and lived into the beginning of the twentieth century. His lifetime spanned a period of notable change, including westward expansion, the Civil War, Reconstruction, and the transition into a modern era.

His death in Bradyville, Cannon County, places him among the Brandon family members who established long-term roots in that community. David G. Brandon's life reflects both endurance and continuity within Middle Tennessee, linking early settlement generations with those that followed.

Benjamin Brandon

Benjamin Brandon

- **Born:** 1817 — Rutherford County, Tennessee, United States
- **Died:** Unknown

Benjamin Brandon was born in Rutherford County during the early years of Tennessee's statehood, placing him within the same early nineteenth-century generation as several other Brandon family members. His life unfolded during a period of settlement, migration, and family expansion across Middle Tennessee.

Although details of his later life remain undocumented, preserving Benjamin Brandon's name ensures continuity within the Brandon family record and leaves space for future clarification as additional records or family knowledge emerge.

Sabella Brandon

Sabella Brandon

- **Born:** 1817 — Rutherford County, Tennessee, United States
- **Died:** 1860 — Hardin County, Tennessee, United States

Sabella Brandon was born in Rutherford County during the early years of Tennessee's statehood and lived during a period of settlement and expansion across the region. Her move later in life to Hardin County reflects the broader internal migration of Tennessee families during the mid-nineteenth century.

Although details of her family role remain limited at present, recording Sabella Brandon preserves an important member of the Brandon family's early nineteenth-century generation and allows for future clarification as additional records emerge.

Hiram Brandon

Hiram Brandon

- **Born:** October 18, 1817 — Cannon County, Tennessee, United States

- **Died:** November 24, 1894 — Checotah, McIntosh County, Oklahoma, United States

Hiram Brandon was born in Cannon County, Tennessee, during the early nineteenth century and lived through a period marked by migration, settlement, and national change. His later move westward and death in McIntosh County, Oklahoma, reflect the broader patterns of expansion and relocation that shaped many American families during the nineteenth century.

His life connects the early Brandon generations of Middle Tennessee with later branches that extended into the western territories, illustrating both continuity of family and adaptability across changing landscapes.

Cornelius Brandon Jr.

Cornelius Brandon Jr.

- **Born:** October 28, 1818 — Rutherford County, Tennessee, United States
- **Died:** 1895 — Cannon County, Tennessee, United States

Cornelius Brandon Jr. was born in Rutherford County during the early nineteenth century and lived into the latter part of that century, a period shaped by settlement, migration, and national transformation. His lifespan covered the years surrounding westward expansion, the Civil War, and Reconstruction.

His later residence and death in Cannon County place him among the Brandon family members who established enduring roots in that area, contributing to the continuity of the Brandon presence in Middle Tennessee across generations.

Louisa Levicy Brandon

Louisa Levicy Brandon

- **Born:** 1822 — Rutherford County, Tennessee, United States
- **Died:** 1910 — Cannon County, Tennessee, United States

Louisa Levicy Brandon was born in Rutherford County during the early nineteenth century and lived well into the early twentieth century. Her long life spanned a period of profound change, including westward expansion, the Civil War, Reconstruction, and the transition into a more modern era.

Her later years in Cannon County place her among the Brandon family members who established deep and lasting roots there, contributing to the continuity of the family's presence in Middle Tennessee across generations.

Calvin C. Brandon

Calvin C. Brandon

- **Born:** 1825 — Rutherford County, Tennessee, United States
- **Died:** February 1, 1904 — Swifton, Jackson County, Arkansas, United States

Calvin C. Brandon was born in Rutherford County, Tennessee, during the early nineteenth century and lived into the opening years of the twentieth century. His lifetime spanned a period of major national change, including westward expansion, the Civil War, Reconstruction, and the settling of new communities beyond Tennessee.

His later residence and death in Jackson County, Arkansas, reflect the migration patterns seen among several members of the Brandon family, as branches of the family moved westward while maintaining ties to their Tennessee roots.

Mary Ann Brandon

Mary Ann Brandon

- **Born:** March 6, 1826 — Rutherford County, Tennessee, United States
- **Died:** May 14, 1897 — Cannon County, Tennessee, United States

Mary Ann Brandon was born in Rutherford County during the early nineteenth century and lived through a lengthy period of change that included westward expansion, the Civil War, and Reconstruction. Her lifetime reflects the experiences of many Tennessee families whose roots remained strong despite national upheaval.

Her death in Cannon County places her among the Brandon family members who maintained long-standing ties to that community, contributing to the continuity of the family's presence in Middle Tennessee across generations.

Rebecca Brandon

Rebecca Brandon

- **Born:** 1829 — Rutherford County, Tennessee, United States
- **Died:** May 14, 1897

Rebecca Brandon was born in Rutherford County during the early nineteenth century and lived through a period marked by settlement, national conflict, and recovery. Her lifetime aligns with other Brandon family members whose lives unfolded across the Civil War era and into the closing years of the nineteenth century.

Although the location of her death is not yet documented, recording Rebecca Brandon preserves an important member of the Brandon family's early Tennessee generation and leaves room for future clarification as additional records emerge.

Jonathan Brandon

Jonathan Brandon

- **Born:** 1832 — Rutherford County, Tennessee, United States
- **Died:** October 25, 1912 — Athabasca Landing, Alberta, Canada

Jonathan Brandon was born in Rutherford County, Tennessee, during the early nineteenth century and lived through a period of dramatic national and continental change. His lifetime spanned the years before and after the Civil War and extended into the early twentieth century.

His later residence and death in Athabasca Landing, Alberta, Canada, mark a significant geographic expansion of the Brandon family line beyond the United States. This movement reflects broader migration patterns of the era, as individuals and families traveled great distances in search of opportunity, land, and new beginnings.

Archibald T. Brandon

Archibald T. Brandon

- **Born:** 1833 — Rutherford County, Tennessee, United States
- **Died:** 1863 — Civil War hospital, Newnan, Coweta County, Georgia

Archibald T. Brandon was born in Rutherford County during the early nineteenth century and came of age as the nation moved toward civil conflict. His death in a Civil War hospital in Newnan, Georgia, places him among the Brandon family members whose lives were directly affected by the war.

His record reflects the personal cost of the conflict and preserves the memory of a generation interrupted by national division and loss.

James Alexander Brandon

James Alexander Brandon

- **Born:** Unknown
- **Died:** Unknown

James Alexander Brandon is recorded as a member of the Brandon family whose life details are presently undocumented. His name reflects nineteenth-century naming patterns common among Tennessee families and suggests placement within the broader early Brandon generations.

Although specific dates and locations are not yet known, preserving his name ensures that this individual remains part of the family record and allows future researchers to attach documentation as it becomes available.

Sibella Brandon

Sibella Brandon

- **Born:** Unknown
- **Died:** Unknown

Sibella Brandon is recorded as a member of the Brandon family whose life details are presently undocumented. Her name appears within the broader Brandon lineage and reflects the naming patterns of the nineteenth century common to Tennessee families.

Although specific dates and locations are not yet known, preserving Sibella Brandon's name ensures she is not lost from the family record and leaves room for future clarification as additional documentation or family knowledge becomes available.

Father of Cornelious:

George B. Brandon Jr.

George B. Brandon

- **Born:** 1732 — Somerset County, Pennsylvania, United States
- **Died:** September 26, 1826 — Union County, South Carolina, United States

George B. Brandon represents the earliest documented generation of the Brandon family currently traced in this line. Born in Pennsylvania during the colonial era, his life reflects the early movement of families southward through the American colonies and into the Carolinas prior to westward expansion into Tennessee.

His later years in Union County, South Carolina, place him among those families who established themselves in the southern backcountry during the eighteenth century. As the father of **Cornelius Brandon**, George B. Brandon stands at the head of the known ancestral path that would later extend into Tennessee and beyond.

Rebecca Neely

Rebecca Neely

- **Born:** 1736 — Rowan County, North Carolina, United States
- **Died:** 1784

Rebecca Neely belonged to the colonial-era generation of American families whose lives unfolded before the founding of the United States. Born in Rowan County, North Carolina, she lived during the time of frontier settlement, family formation, and early migration through the southern colonies.

As the wife of **George B. Brandon**, Rebecca Neely was part of the foundational family unit that gave rise to the Brandon line, which was later established in South Carolina and Tennessee. Her early death in 1784 places her life entirely within the pre-Revolutionary and Revolutionary period, marking her as one of the earliest maternal ancestors in this documented lineage.

Children:

George Brandon III

George Brandon III

- **Born:** August 2, 1770 — Rowan County, North Carolina, United States
- **Died:** May 12, 1844 — Rutherford County, North Carolina, United States

George Brandon III was born in Rowan County, North Carolina, during the colonial era and lived into the mid-nineteenth century. His lifetime spanned the Revolutionary period, the early years of the United States, and the westward movement that followed independence.

His residence and death in Rutherford County, North Carolina, place him firmly within the Carolina roots of the Brandon family, representing a generation that remained in the region while later descendants moved south into South Carolina and west into Tennessee.

Sybella Brandon

Sybella Brandon

- **Born:** 1772 — Sumner County, Tennessee, United States

- **Died:** Rowan County, North Carolina, United States *(date unknown)*

Sybella Brandon was born in the late eighteenth century, placing her within the colonial and early American generation of the Brandon family. Her lifetime aligns with the period following the American Revolution, when families moved between North Carolina and the early Tennessee frontier.

Her death in Rowan County, North Carolina, reflects the back-and-forth movement of families during this era, as kinship ties and settlement patterns often spanned multiple colonies and early states.

Cornelius Brandon

Cornelius Brandon

- **Born:** 1783 — Rowan County, North Carolina, United States
- **Died:** December 11, 1852 — Cannon County, Tennessee, United States

Cornelius Brandon represents the pivotal generation that carried the Brandon family from the Carolinas into Middle Tennessee. Born in Rowan County, North Carolina, he came of age during the early years of the United States and lived through a period of migration and settlement that shaped the family's long-term geographic identity.

By adulthood, Cornelius had relocated westward into Tennessee, where he spent his later years in Cannon County. His life marks the transition from colonial and early American roots into the firmly established Tennessee branches that followed through his descendants.

Family Connections

- **Father:** George B. Brandon (1732–1826)
- **Mother:** Rebecca Neely (1736–1784)
- **Spouse:** Mary Phoebe Tennison (1787–1866)
- **Son:** Abraham Brandon (1811–1896)

Father of Geroge Brandon Jr.:

George William Brandon Sr.

George William Brandon Sr.

- **Born:** 1702 — Yohoghany, Westmoreland County, Pennsylvania, United States
- **Died:** December 14, 1772 — Rowan County, North Carolina, British Colonial America

George William Brandon Sr. represents the earliest known ancestor in the documented Brandon line presented in this volume. Born in colonial Pennsylvania at the opening of the eighteenth century, his life reflects the movement of early families southward through the American colonies during a period of frontier settlement and expansion.

By later life, George William Brandon Sr. had settled in Rowan County, North Carolina, where he died prior to the American Revolution. His lifetime unfolded entirely within the colonial era, making him the foundational patriarch from whom subsequent Brandon generations would descend through the Carolinas and into Tennessee.

Mary Ann Marian Armstrong

Mary Ann Marian Armstrong

- **Born:** 1704
- **Died:** July 29, 1755 — Rowan County, North Carolina, United States

Mary Ann Marian Armstrong belonged to the early colonial generation of families who settled the southern backcountry during the first half of the eighteenth century. Living entirely within the colonial era, her life predates the American Revolution and reflects the endurance and adaptability required of families establishing new communities on the frontier.

As the wife of **George William Brandon Sr.**, Mary Ann Marian Armstrong stands at the maternal head of the Brandon lineage documented in this volume. Through her children, the family line continued through North Carolina and later expanded into South Carolina and Tennessee, forming the roots of generations that followed.

Children:

Mary Catherine Brandon

Mary Catherine Brandon

- **Born:** 1731 — Huntington, Lancaster County, Pennsylvania, United States
- **Died:** November 21, 1814 — Union County, South Carolina, United States of America

Mary Catherine Brandon was born in colonial Pennsylvania during the early eighteenth century and lived through a period of migration and settlement that shaped the southern backcountry. Her lifetime spanned the years before and after the American Revolution, placing her among the earliest documented generations of the Brandon family in America.

Her later life in Union County, South Carolina, aligns with the movement of Brandon family members from Pennsylvania through the Carolinas prior to their westward expansion into Tennessee. Preserving her record strengthens the maternal presence within the colonial-era Brandon lineage.

George B. Brandon

George B. Brandon

- **Born:** 1732 — Somerset County, Pennsylvania, United States
- **Died:** September 26, 1826 — Union County, South Carolina, United States

George B. Brandon was born in colonial Pennsylvania during the early eighteenth century and lived through a period of significant migration and settlement in British North America. His life reflects the southward movement of families from Pennsylvania into the Carolina backcountry during the decades preceding the American Revolution.

By later life, George B. Brandon had settled in Union County, South Carolina, where he spent his final years. His lifetime bridged the colonial era, the Revolutionary period, and the early years of the United States. As the father of Cornelius Brandon, he stands as a critical generational link between the earliest Brandon ancestors and the Tennessee-based generations that followed.

Christopher A. Brandon

Christopher A. Brandon

- **Born:** February 10, 1738 — Monaghan, York County, Pennsylvania, United States
- **Died:** November 26, 1806 — Rowan County, North Carolina, United States

Christopher A. Brandon was born in colonial Pennsylvania during the mid-eighteenth century and lived through the American Revolutionary period into the early years of the United States. His life reflects the migration of families southward from Pennsylvania into the Carolina backcountry during a time of frontier settlement and expansion.

His death in Rowan County, North Carolina, places him firmly within the same regional setting as other early Brandon family members, marking continuity in the Carolina roots of the family prior to later westward movement into Tennessee.

William Brandon

William Brandon

- **Born:** 1739 — Hanover, Dauphin County, Pennsylvania, United States
- **Died:** June 25, 1781 — Cleveland County, North Carolina, United States

William Brandon was born in colonial Pennsylvania during the mid-eighteenth century and lived during the turbulent years surrounding the American Revolution. His life reflects the movement of families from Pennsylvania into the Carolina backcountry as frontier communities expanded southward.

His death in North Carolina in 1781 places him squarely within the Revolutionary era, marking him as part of the generation whose lives were shaped directly by colonial conflict, migration, and the struggle for independence.

Abraham Brandon (1742–1802)

Abraham Brandon

- **Born:** 1742 — Monaghan, York County, Pennsylvania, United States

- **Died:** February 5, 1802 — Rowan County, North Carolina, United States

Abraham Brandon was born in colonial Pennsylvania during the mid-eighteenth century and later settled in Rowan County, North Carolina. His life spanned the years leading up to and following the American Revolution, placing him among the generation that experienced the transition from British colonial rule to the early United States.

Although not part of the direct ancestral line traced in this volume, Abraham Brandon represents an important **collateral branch** of the Brandon family. Recording his life preserves the broader family context surrounding the primary lineage and helps distinguish parallel branches within the colonial Brandon generations.

John Brandon (1742–1758)

John Brandon

- **Born:** May 9, 1742 — Huntington Township, Lancaster County, Pennsylvania
- **Died:** January 25, 1758

John Brandon was born in colonial Pennsylvania during the early eighteenth century and died in childhood. His short life occurred during a period of frontier settlement and hardship, when infant and childhood mortality was common among colonial families.

Although his life was brief, recording John Brandon preserves an important member of the Brandon family's earliest known generation and helps document the full household structure of the colonial-era Brandon family.

James Brandon (1745–1789)

James Brandon

- **Born:** 1745 — Cumberland Township, Bucks County, Pennsylvania, United States
- **Died:** 1789 — Venango County, Pennsylvania, United States

James Brandon was born in colonial Pennsylvania during the mid-eighteenth century and lived through the years surrounding the American Revolution. His lifetime reflects the movement and uncertainty of families living on the Pennsylvania frontier during a period of conflict, settlement, and political transformation.

His death in Venango County places him among those Brandon family members who remained in Pennsylvania rather than migrating south into the Carolinas, representing a **parallel colonial branch** of the family.

Mary Brandon (1746–1803)

Mary Brandon

- **Born:** 1746 — Rowan County, North Carolina
- **Died:** 1803 — Gallatin, Sumner County, Tennessee

Mary Brandon was born in Rowan County, North Carolina, during the colonial era and later migrated westward into Tennessee, reflecting the early movement of families beyond the Carolinas following the American Revolution. Her death in Gallatin, Sumner County, places her among the Brandon family members who helped establish early roots in Middle Tennessee.

Although not part of the direct ancestral line, Mary Brandon represents an important **collateral branch** of the Brandon family. Her life helps document the broader family network that surrounded and supported the primary lineage as it expanded across multiple colonies and states.

Eleanor Brandon (1748–1774)

Eleanor Brandon

- **Born:** 1748 — Rowan County, North Carolina
- **Died:** May 4, 1774 — York, York County, Pennsylvania, United States

Eleanor Brandon was born in Rowan County, North Carolina, during the colonial era and died at an early age prior to the American Revolution. Her movement northward to Pennsylvania reflects the fluid migration patterns of eighteenth-century families, whose lives often crossed colonial boundaries in search of opportunity or kinship connections.

Although her life was brief, Eleanor Brandon's record preserves an important member of the extended Brandon family and helps complete the picture of the colonial household surrounding the direct ancestral line.

Sidney Brandon (1750–1818)

Sidney Brandon

- **Born:** 1750 — Rowan County, North Carolina
- **Died:** May 4, 1818 — Rutherford County, North Carolina

Sidney Brandon was born in Rowan County during the colonial period and lived through the American Revolution and into the early years of the United States. Her life reflects the continuity of the Brandon family in North Carolina during a time of political change and regional growth.

Her death in Rutherford County places her firmly within the Carolina heartland of the Brandon family, representing a generation that remained rooted in the region while later descendants moved westward into Tennessee and beyond.

Father of George William Brandon:

John Richard Brandon 1st

John Richard Brandon

- **Born:** 1672
- **Died:** 1716

John Richard Brandon is recognized as the **earliest known Brandon ancestor to arrive in America**, marking the beginning of the Brandon family's presence in the Americas. Living during the late seventeenth and early eighteenth centuries, his life unfolded entirely within the colonial period, before the formation of the United States.

As the founding American ancestor of this Brandon line, John Richard Brandon stands at the head of a lineage that would span centuries, crossing colonies and states—from colonial settlements through Pennsylvania and the Carolinas, and later into Tennessee and beyond. His arrival laid the foundation for every generation of the Brandon family that followed on American soil.

Mary Ann Armstrong

Mary Ann Armstrong

- **Born:** May 19, 1665 — London, London, England, United Kingdom

- **Died:** 1702 — Somerset County, Pennsylvania, USA

Mary Ann Armstrong was born in London during the mid-seventeenth century, a time of political upheaval and transformation in England. Her life spanned the final decades of the Old World before the Brandon family's transition to the American colonies.

By the end of her life, Mary Ann Armstrong had crossed the Atlantic to colonial America, dying in Pennsylvania in 1702. Her journey represents the earliest known migration in this family line and marks the **bridge between England and America** for the Brandon legacy.

As the mother within the earliest generation documented in this work, Mary Ann Armstrong stands at the head of the maternal line that would give rise to the Brandon family's centuries-long presence in America.

Children:

John Richard Brandon

John Richard Brandon

- **Born:** 1691 — Middlesex (later Greater London), England
- **Died:** May 15, 1756 — Salisbury, Rowan County, North Carolina, United States of America

John Richard Brandon represents the **first confirmed generation of the Brandon family to establish roots in colonial America**. Born in Middlesex, England, during the late seventeenth century, he lived through a period of significant migration as families left England for opportunity and stability in the Americas.

By adulthood, John Richard Brandon had crossed the Atlantic and settled in colonial North Carolina, where he spent his later years in Salisbury, Rowan County. His life bridges the Old World and the Americas, marking the beginning of the Brandon family's enduring presence in America.

As the immigrant ancestor of this line, John Richard Brandon stands at the head of a lineage that would expand through the Carolinas, Pennsylvania, Tennessee, and beyond over the centuries that followed.

James Brandon (1693–1758)

James Brandon

- **Born:** 1693 — Middlesex, London, England
- **Died:** May 12, 1758 — Huntington, Adams County, Pennsylvania, United States

James Brandon was born in Middlesex, England, during the late seventeenth century and later migrated to colonial America, becoming part of the earliest Brandon presence in the Americas. His life spans the period of English emigration to the American colonies and the establishment of family lines in Pennsylvania.

His death in Pennsylvania places him among the first Brandon family members to settle north of the Carolinas, representing an early branching of the family within the colonies. Preserving his record helps document the full scope of Brandon migration patterns during the colonial period.

George William Brandon Sr.

George William Brandon Sr.

- **Born:** 1702 — Yohoghany, Westmoreland County, Pennsylvania, United States

- **Died:** December 14, 1772 — Rowan County, North Carolina, British Colonial America

George William Brandon Sr. belongs to the first fully American-born generation of the Brandon family. Born in colonial Pennsylvania at the beginning of the eighteenth century, his life reflects the early movement of families from the northern colonies into the southern back country.

By later life, he had settled in Rowan County, North Carolina, where he died prior to the American Revolution. His lifetime unfolded entirely within the colonial era, bridging the immigrant generation from England with the generations that would expand throughout the Carolinas and eventually into Tennessee.

George William Brandon Sr. stands as a foundational patriarch in the Brandon family's American history, anchoring the lineage firmly on American soil.

Family Connections

- **Father:** John Richard Brandon (1691–1756), born in England

- **Mother:** Mary Ann Armstrong (1665–1702), born in London, England
- **Son:** George B. Brandon (1732–1826)

- # From the Old World to the Present Day

- The Brandon family story begins across the Atlantic, in England, during the closing years of the seventeenth century. With courage and resolve, the earliest Brandon ancestors crossed into the Americas, seeking opportunity, stability, and a future for those who would follow. From their first American foothold, the family moved steadily through the colonies—into Pennsylvania, the Carolinas, and eventually westward into Tennessee—following the same paths taken by countless early American families.
- Generation by generation, the Brandons established roots, raised families, worked the land, and endured the trials of frontier life, war, and national change. Their legacy was not shaped by titles or heraldry, but by perseverance, faith, and the bonds of family. Through migration, settlement, and service, the Brandon name became firmly woven into the American story.
- Today, the descendants of these early Brandon settlers remain—living across the United States and beyond—carrying forward the lives, values, and memories of those who came before them. This record stands as both a remembrance of the past and a gift to future

generations, ensuring that the journey of the Brandon family—from its beginnings abroad to its presence today—will not be forgotten.

The Brandon line continues

www.ingramcontent.com/pod-product-compliance
Lightning Source LLC
LaVergne TN
LVHW041617070526
838199LV00052B/3177